THE STARTUP ROADMAP

21 STEPS TO PROFITABILITY

THE STARTUP ROADMAP

21 STEPS TO PROFITABILITY

By Ed McLaughlin
Wyn Lydecker
and Paul McLaughlin

BLUE
SUNSETS
BOOKS

Published in the United States by Blue Sunsets Books, an imprint of Blue Sunsets LLC, Darien, CT
www.bluesunsets.com

Blue Sunsets Books are available at special discounts for bulk purchases for sales promotions or corporate use. Special editions, including personalized covers, excerpts of existing books, or books with corporate logos, can be created in large quantities for special needs. For more information, contact the authors at: ed@thepurposeisprofit.com.

Library of Congress Control Number: 2015905981
Blue Sunsets LLC, Darien, CT

ISBN: 978-0-9863043-2-3
eISBN: 978-0-9863043-3-0

PRINTED IN THE UNITED STATES

The Startup Roadmap Book & Cover Design by Pat Scully Design

The Startup Roadmap: 21 Steps to Profitability

TABLE OF CONTENTS

THE STARTUP ROADMAP

21 STEPS TO PROFITABILITY

ABOUT THE STARTUP ROADMAP

The Startup Roadmap was designed with one purpose in mind: to improve your probability of startup success. The Roadmap is a step-by-step guide designed to help you understand the mechanics of starting and running a profitable new business.

Please feel free to contact us with questions and recommendations for improvement. We can be reached via email at: ed@thepurposeisprofit.com.

If you believe The Startup Roadmap can help your friends fulfill their entrepreneurial goals, please recommend it to them. By the way, The Startup Roadmap will be included in our book, *The Purpose Is Profit*, scheduled to be released in January 2016.

We wish you success in building your business. Please let us know how you are doing.

Sincerely,

Ed, Wyn, and Paul
www.thepurposeisprofit.com

THE STARTUP ROADMAP

You know you want to start a business, but you are not sure how to do it. Like many entrepreneurs, you are chomping at the bit to lift off, but you are struggling with a healthy fear of failure. You need a step-by-step process to guide you through the uncertainties of starting up. If you are determined to build, lead, and grow a profitable business, *The Startup Roadmap* is designed for you.

You need a way to filter your ideas and figure out if they are bankable, sustainable, and worthy of your time, money, and reputation. You want to get started, but you do not want to take unnecessary risks. As much as possible, you want to look ahead and figure things out before you take the plunge – but you do not want to lose momentum, hamper your creativity, your energy, or your enthusiasm to get started – for fear you never will.

As I see it, you have a choice. You can invest the time upfront to plan your journey, or you can roll the dice and launch without a plan, figuring out the inevitable problems and challenges as they present themselves. While I understand the need to pivot and make adjustments as you develop your business, I am not as confident in the concept of repeatedly trying, failing, and restarting, given the risks and costs to your livelihood. I believe you need to think through the essential steps to profitability before you launch.

A study by Harvard Business School senior lecturer Shikhar Ghosh showed that 75% of venture capital-backed startups fail and that non-venture capital-backed businesses fail at an even greater rate. To improve your probability of success, you need a means for exploring, testing, and validating ideas – one that builds your confidence that you are moving in the right direction before you start up. That's why I have developed *The Startup Roadmap*.

When I created the plans to launch my own business, USI, I followed a similar process. I could not afford to fail. I had a young family that relied on my income. Even though I couldn't wait to go out on my own, I had to consider the ramifications of leaving my corporate job. Prior to liftoff, my team and I invested six months of our time – without compensation – in careful speculation, answering the 21 questions included in *The Startup Roadmap*. It paid big dividends. We grew USI into an Inc. 500 company and then sold it 14 years later to Johnson Controls, a Fortune 100 company.

I want to share this Roadmap with you to help put you and your business on the path to long-term profit and success.

21 Steps to Profitability

The 21 steps in *The Startup Roadmap* fall into three categories: Proof, Profit, and Potential. First, you need to develop and prove your idea. Second, you have to figure out if you can make a profit. And third, you need to assess the business's potential for growth.

Section 1: Proof

Step 1 │ **Business Idea:** *Can you state your business idea clearly and concisely?* If you cannot reduce your idea to a few simple, understandable sentences, then it may be too complex. And it will certainly be too hard to explain to potential customers, partners, and investors.

Before I launched, I talked to prospective customers and advisors to test and explain my business concept. I boiled down my idea into a single summary sentence: "We will become a corporation's single source of management for all their real estate needs." A corporation could outsource their entire real estate department to my new business, USI. Even though it was a novel concept, it clicked with my stakeholders right away.

To develop and hone your business idea, ask yourself:

■ Why are you starting this business?

■ What is the purpose of your new business?

■ What product or service will you deliver?

■ How is your business different?

■ Will your stakeholders easily understand your idea?

A clear, crisp and concise description of your business will help you acquire customers and build your brand.

Step 2 │ **Distinctive Competence:** *What unique experience, skills, and knowledge do you bring to your business?* If you can identify an unserved need for a product or service in an industry where you have distinctive competence, you could have a bankable business. You could minimize the risks by utilizing your knowledge of existing models, customers, customer needs, pricing, and competition.

I struggled for years pondering the type of business to start, its potential for profit, and the cost of possible failure. I thought through hundreds of scenarios and the associated risks, when one day, it struck me: The answer to all of these questions was distinctive competence.

When I looked back on my past successes, they had one thing in common: I had some combination of tried-and-true experience and a track record of accomplishment that enabled me to succeed. This mixture of experience and expertise defined my distinctive competence. I believed that if I built my new business around my distinctive competence I could substantially improve the probability of future success. The same principles apply to you.

If you believe you have a breakthrough business idea, then you will need the experience and the expertise to execute it. If you do not possess the necessary knowledge or skill to carry out your idea, you will need to hire or partner with someone who does.

Answer the following questions to determine your unique competence:

- What special knowledge, talent, or skill do you have?
- Do you have a track record of success in a particular field?
- How can you apply your talent to your new business?
- What additional competencies do you need to succeed?
- How can you fill the competency void with partners, team members, technology, tools, and/or education?

Challenging yourself to answer these questions will fortify your startup success.

Step 3 | **Product Description:** *Can you succinctly describe the product you will sell, who will use it, and the problem it will solve?* It is critical to be able to articulate your product's features, its position in the marketplace, and its competitive advantage.

Traditionally, real estate transactions were handled entirely by local brokers, individual deal by individual deal. The market needed a more efficient process to get work done. Outsourcing was the answer. USI described its service as the outsourced manager of a corporation's real estate portfolio. USI became the customer's single point of contact for all their transaction and information needs. We promised to reduce occupancy costs, while rebating a share of the commissions to offset overall service delivery expenses. We hadn't thought of every service we could offer from the beginning, but we had a vision for selling a full suite of integrated services.

When starting out, you need to focus on the basics of your product's attributes, its position in the marketplace, and its profit potential, while keeping your ultimate vision in mind.

Answer the following questions to help develop your product description:

- What is your product or service?
- How will it be used, and who will use it?
- What problem will your product solve?
- What are your product's features?
- How is your product positioned in the market?
- What are your product's competitive advantages?
- How will your product evolve?
- Will you be offering a family of integrated products?

A clear and concise product description will enhance sales, improve product development, and create a platform for future product offerings.

Step 4 | **Market Opportunity:** *What industry are you entering, and what are its trends?* Define the industry and the segment you will target. Recognize that the greatest opportunities lie in industry sectors that are growing and changing.

In my case, corporate real estate was undergoing dramatic change, creating significant opportunity. The mantra of the day was: Do more with less. The practice of outsourcing non-core service areas was beginning to take off. Corporations were saving millions by hiring outsourced providers with specialized expertise to reduce costs, enhance productivity, and improve service to customers.

My idea was to provide a service that would lead the outsourcing wave in corporate real estate. My business would enable companies to outsource the management of their real estate portfolios and a host of related services.

To define your market and the opportunity, you should invest the time to answer all of the following questions:

- What industry is your business in?
- What sector of the industry are you targeting?
- What changes are taking place?
- How does your product address the changes?
- How can your product create change?
- What is the size of the opportunity?
- What is the rate of growth of the target sector?
- What trends will impact the rate of growth?

Answering these questions may take some research. While you do the research, remember that it is important to stay at a high level. You don't want to get mired in minutia. All of your answers should be available to you through online sources, industry groups, libraries, competitors, and business owners in the same sector.

Step 5 | Target Customer: *Do you have a clear understanding of who will buy your product and why?* You need to be able to describe your target customer and their need for your product. You need to understand your customer's goals, motivations, budget, demographics, and characteristics, as well as their role and responsibility within the buying organization or household.

For USI, I knew my target customers were the chief financial officers (CFOs) and real estate executives (CREs) of corporations with substantial real estate holdings. They were in control of the budget and the real estate. Fortunately, I knew the industry inside and out, understood how it worked, and recognized what the CFOs and CREs were seeking. There was substantial opportunity for cost reduction and improved asset management. In most cases, real estate was – and still is – the second highest overhead expense, right after personnel costs.

Figure out how well you know your target customer by completing the following checklist:

- Who is the target customer for your product?
  - Goals and motivations
  - Demographic description
  - Unique characteristics
- What is your customer's role and responsibility?

▪ Why does your customer need your product?

▪ What motivates your customer to buy your product?

▪ How does your customer influence the buying decision?

▪ Does your customer control the budget?

▪ How does your target customer measure success?

The best way to develop a profitable new business is through a comprehensive understanding of your target customer.

Step 6 | **Value Proposition:** *What is your product's unique benefit, and how does that benefit meet a critical customer need?* The best value proposition clearly defines and quantifies how your product will solve a problem or relieve a customer's pain better than anything else.

The most efficient path to profit is a value proposition that succinctly explains the benefits and rewards your customer will derive from a relationship with your company. My experience has shown that a value proposition which provides a crystal clear quantification of benefits is easiest to sell and the most compelling to buy. A business-to-business (B2B) value proposition is dominated by quantified benefits, whereas a business-to-consumer (B2C) value proposition leans more heavily on qualitative benefits.

When I was thinking about USI, I knew our value proposition would be our competitive differentiator. Since our competitors sold their products based on their brand names, using a traditional approach to sell and deliver their service, the doorway was wide open for change. I was confident we would have a bankable value proposition if we could demonstrate how our target customers could receive quantified benefits many times greater than the cost they paid. USI's value proposition was so well received that it propelled USI to a 40% compounded annual growth rate.

Define Quantitative Benefits (Typically B2B)

To develop your B2B value proposition and generate a clear picture of your quantitative benefits, you should answer the following questions.

How much can your product:

■ Increase your customer's revenues?

■ Decrease your customer's expenses?

■ Contribute to your customer's profits?

■ Improve your customer's productivity?

■ Reduce your customer's cycle time?

■ Improve your customer's supply chain?

■ Improve access to critical information?

Once my partners and I had nailed down the hard benefits of our product, we also enumerated the qualitative benefits including higher quality service, improved employee morale, enhanced customer satisfaction, etc. You need to compile a list of both quantitative and qualitative benefits for your B2B product.

Define Qualitative Benefits (Typically B2C)

To define your B2C product's benefit(s), ask questions that center on alleviating pain or providing a distinct advantage for your customer. Narrow down your unique qualitative benefits by asking if your B2C product will do any of the following:

■ Make life more convenient?

- Provide safety or security?

- Increase self-esteem or confidence?

- Improve the quality of life?

- Improve health?

Once you determine and describe your product's qualitative benefits, you should also specify the quantitative benefits of your B2C product, such as saving time and money.

Step 7 | Competitive Advantage: *What differentiates your business from the competition?* You can identify your competitive advantage by comparing and contrasting your value proposition against the value propositions of your finest competitors. This process will set your business apart by pinpointing the genuine elements of differentiation between you and your competitors.

Your competitive differentiation can come from any number of sources. USI had a multi-faceted competitive advantage. Even though I knew I would be competing with my former employer, I intended to go after a different segment of the market. My former employer focused on the Fortune 100, while USI would target the middle of the Fortune 1000. In our market segment, we had the first-mover advantage with a sustainable, innovative business model: a new way for corporations to manage their real estate portfolios through outsourcing.

Based on your competitive research, you should be able to generate a list of your competitors, along with their value propositions. This information will give you a picture of the competitive landscape, allowing you to identify your truly unique advantages.

You can identify your competitive advantage by completing the following steps:

1. List your competitors and their value propositions

2. Compare your value proposition to your competitors'

3. Answer the following questions to determine your unique advantages vs your competition:

   ■ Does your product fill a gap in the market?

   ■ Do you have a first-mover advantage?

   ■ Is your product innovative?

   ■ Is your product disruptive vs traditional models?

   ■ Are you using technology as a competitive weapon?

   ■ Do you have control of your intellectual property?

   ■ Do you have a unique talent or special reputation?

   ■ Does your product improve customer productivity?

   ■ Does your product increase customer revenues?

   ■ Does your product save your customer money?

4. Determine if your competitive advantage is sustainable.

Pinpointing your competitive differentiation will crystallize your genuine advantages vs the competition.

Step 8 | **Pre-Orders: *Can you secure pre-orders from your target customers?*** A pre-order is an informal commitment from customers to purchase your product before it is formally offered to the market. Pre-orders are vital to any new business because they validate your business idea before you launch.

Like many entrepreneurs forming B2B startups, I had the advantage of a significant, pre-existing corporate relationship base to build on. My reputation put me well ahead of the game in lining up pre-orders. In a few cases, my customer relationships were close enough that I could try out my idea informally. It turned out that this would be the way I would secure my first pre-orders. That gave me the confidence to leave my job and launch my business. Looking back, I realize that my pre-orders were the key factor that led to achieving profitability in USI's fourth month of operation.

Securing pre-sales is the single most important point of validation and vitality for a new business. If you can line up enough pre-orders, you can maximize control of your company and minimize the need for outside funding.

To secure pre-orders:

- Generate a target list of high-trust contacts and likely buyers of your new product

- Internalize your value proposition and be able to articulate it clearly and concisely when you meet with prospects

- Contact your closest customers – ones whom you trust – and ask them if they would place an order with your startup

- Approach trusted advisors and ask them to make introductions to prospective customers

- Sell your competitive advantages to clearly delineate your product in the mind of your customer

- Close for the pre-order and document the mutual commitment to do business together.

Secure as many pre-orders as you can reasonably fill on time, on budget, and at the quality level your customer expects. Keep in mind that your reputation for fulfilling your commitments is your number one asset.

Section Two: Profit

Step 9 | **Business Model:** *How will you make money?* The business model explains how you will pull together and manage all the component parts of your business to create value for your customers and yourself. Your business model includes your revenue generation plan, product pricing, production and distribution, use of technology, marketing and sales, resource requirements, and profit validation.

Too often entrepreneurs fall in love with their idea but fail to have a business model worked out that will make a profit and generate sustainable cash flow.

When I had worked at Trammell Crow Company, the Vice President of Real Estate at Baxter Healthcare and I developed the business engine to outsource hundreds of transactions and construction projects. This was the first time real estate services were outsourced. The concept was completely innovative. Because I had worked so intimately on developing the business model, I knew the math involved and felt certain of the huge profit potential a similar model could generate for a new outsourcing business.

The Profit section of *The Startup Roadmap* includes the eight major components of the business model. These components are listed below and discussed in detail in Steps #10 through #17.

Step #10: Revenue Generation

Step #11: Product Pricing

Step #12: Production & Distribution

Step #13: Creative Use of Technology

Step #14: Marketing

Step #15: Sales

Step #16: Resource Requirements

Step #17: Profit Validation

Please do not underestimate the importance of a sound business model and all of its component parts on your ability to create value and generate profit.

Step 10 | Revenue Generation: *How will you generate revenue?* A key step in developing your revenue model is determining the types and sources of revenue your business will generate. Revenue types include product sales, service fees, advertising sales, data access fees, license fees, and/or commissions.

Each type of revenue generated can come from a multitude of sources. For example, sources of revenue from service sales can vary depending on customer type and category including online, mobile, consumer, corporate, institutional, and/or government. Additionally, each category can expand into multiple sources. For example, the corporate sales category can include major accounts, named accounts, vertical markets, geographic territories, partnerships, and one-off sales.

USI had a pretty simple revenue model. We sold real estate portfolio management and transaction management services to corporations. Our customers paid us fees for dedicated resources and commissions on transactions. As the business evolved and our service lines expanded, we developed a more complex fee structure suited to the types of services our customers consumed.

How will you structure your revenue model?

■ Will you collect sales revenue directly from customers in exchange for the service or product?

- Will your business act as an intermediary, helping to bring buyers and sellers together, and collecting a fee for the service or a commission on the resulting sale?

- Will your business be a publisher of content or the creator of an online community that charges for access to the content or community?

- Will you provide content or community for free and collect revenues from advertisers who want to target your readers or users?

- Will you give permission for your product to be used in exchange for a license fee?

- Will you be a collector of data and charge fees to marketers for access to that information?

- Will your business use a combination of these revenue models?

Determining the types and sources of revenue your business will generate is the first step toward realizing a profit.

Step 11 | **Product Pricing: *What will you charge for your product?*** The revenue model you choose, combined with your product's positioning in the marketplace and your profit target will help you determine your price. Each type of revenue model will most likely have market benchmarks you can research to help you price competitively.

From my previous corporate sales experience, I had a firm understanding of traditional pricing models for real estate services. By aggregating portfolio and transaction services through a single source, I knew I could cover my costs and beat the competition with aggressive volume-based pricing. If you know your industry, you may be able to do the same. But first consider the following questions:

- Will you be developing a radical new pricing model?

- Will your price be aligned with traditional benchmarks?

- Will your price be competitive?

- Will you be selling a premium product, enabling you to charge more than your competitors, or will you undercut the competition?

- Should you use a simple markup to cover your unit costs?

- If you are a content provider, what are the prevailing rates for the type of advertising you are selling?

- If you are a provider of data, what do marketers typically pay for access to similar information?

- Will your price cover your cost and leave room for a reasonable profit?

Once you can explain the basic revenue model and your pricing, you can estimate how many customers you expect to have, how many sales you'll likely make to each one, and how often you will make those sales – daily, weekly, monthly, annually. Taken together, this information will enable you to project your total revenue.

Step 12 | Production and Distribution: *What will it take to create, manufacture, and deliver your product to your customers?* For a manufactured product, you will need to think through and quantify your requirements for raw materials, labor, machinery, inventory, and distribution. For a service business, you will need to quantify your service fulfillment costs including staffing, travel costs, response times, and performance reporting.

Since USI was a service business, we were concerned about sales and service delivery costs. Beyond the production of proposals and due-diligence binders, we did not have a manufacturing cost. The key components of our product were account management, data management, market knowledge and negotiation skills. USI's expenses were very similar to a traditional consulting business with most of our employees situated on-site at our customers' headquarters.

On the other hand, a manufacturing and distribution business has a more significant challenge in accurately estimating production costs. It will be important to develop a thorough production cost model to ensure you have considered all of the major costs. Some of the factors you will need to address to estimate production costs include the following:

Prototype costs:

- How will you create a prototype or samples to help you secure pre-orders?

- How much will it cost to create a prototype or sample products?

Production costs:

- Quantify the type, amount, and source of materials, labor and equipment needed to manufacture your product

- Generate a preliminary estimate of costs for materials, labor, and/or equipment needed for your product

- Determine whether you will make your product or outsource

- If you make your product:
  - What are your raw material costs?
  - What are your labor costs?

— What are your equipment costs?

— What are your facilities costs?

— What are your distribution costs?

— How long will it take to manufacture your product?

■ What is the total unit production cost of your product?

■ If you outsource, who will make your product, how much will it cost, and how long will it take?

■ Finalize the make-vs-buy decision by weighing the quantitative and qualitative benefits of each.

Determining accurate production costs and time frames for a manufacturing business is critical to the development of a profitable and reliable business model. Please keep in mind that this is merely a high-level outline designed to get you started.

Step 13 | Creative Use of Technology: *How will you leverage technology to streamline your operations, improve customer service, and open up new revenue lines?* Intelligent use of technology can create a distinct competitive advantage, tighten your relationship with customers, improve access to critical information, and generate a recurring profit stream.

When I was thinking through my business model, I planned on applying my high-tech background from my early career at both IBM and HP to the low-tech world of real estate. I understood the value of systems integration and believed that a similar approach could be used to manage the incredible variety of information and relationships within corporate real estate. Systems integration turned out to be a distinguishing characteristic of our business model, ultimately creating a new service sector that opened the door for USI to offer even more benefits to our customers.

We developed a proprietary software solution named Sequentra to serve the corporate real estate market. We created a wholly separate brand and housed it within a new company named Sequentra Solutions Inc. We used Sequentra as one of our strategic weapons. Our software enabled workflows, improved access to critical information, and tightened our link with the customer.

Here are some of the questions you should consider when applying technology to your business:

■ How can you utilize technology to differentiate your offering?

■ How can you develop software applications that provide critical decision support information and new revenue streams?

■ How can you apply technology to streamline work processes?

■ How can you utilize technology to tighten the link with your customers?

■ How can you utilize technology to create a sustainable competitive advantage?

■ How can you utilize technology to revolutionize your industry?

Today, the technology platforms available are growing exponentially, and with them, the opportunities to create businesses of incredible lasting value. If you are not the tech person in your business, make sure you invest in finding a good one.

Step 14 | **Marketing: *How will you create awareness and persuade customers to buy your product?*** As a startup, you need a plan to reach and educate your target customers about the benefits of your value proposition without spending a lot of money. Establish a meaningful budget, implement your marketing plan, and measure your plan based on tangible results.

Successful marketing depends upon determining the most cost-effective means to communicate your value proposition to your target customer. Since we had a finite list of target customers – the CFOs and CREs of the Fortune 1000 – we decided the best way to motivate interest in our company was to communicate a consistent message of success. The primary goal of our early marketing efforts was to create a receptive audience for our sales force.

First, we needed to notify our target market that we existed – announcing the formation and purpose of USI. Second, we had to raise awareness of our value proposition – especially how we were different from our competitors. Third, we needed to bombard our target market with consistent monthly announcements of our achievements. We wanted our target audience to feel as though they were missing something of value if they did not meet with us.

Since we had a finite audience, we needed point-to-point marketing, not mass media. At the time, we used direct mail. Nowadays, we would have developed a targeted email campaign, supplemented with social media, all connected through a closed-loop system utilizing our website and mobile applications.

Successful businesses connect with their customers on multiple levels and in numerous dimensions, the scope of which is subject to cost constraints. The following components should be part of your marketing mix:

■ Website	■ Online Advertising
■ Social Media	■ Mobile
■ Direct Email	■ Promotions

■ Collateral   ■ Events

■ Public Relations   ■ CRM Systems

When putting your marketing plan together, it's important to remember that everything should flow from your value proposition. You cannot develop an effective marketing plan unless you know your target customer, their needs, and how your product satisfies their needs. Some of the most important questions you should address in your marketing plan include:

1. What are the most cost-effective ways to build awareness of your new venture with your target customers?

2. How can you communicate your value proposition to your target customers?

3. How can you secure permission from your target customers to utilize their email address for direct marketing?

4. How can you design a cost-effective, non-obtrusive way to keep your target customer informed of your success?

5. How can you persuade and influence your target customer to buy from you?

Be careful not to undervalue the role of marketing in your startup. You have made a decision to start a new company, and you are confident in your value proposition. Make sure your target customers know that you exist and educate them on the benefits of your value proposition.

Step 15 | Sales: *How will you secure hard orders from your target customers?* Your sales team is responsible for connecting directly with the customer for the purpose of solving problems, tailoring solutions, making proposals, and closing orders. Will you build a direct sales force, develop a call center, create an e-commerce platform, or outsource the sales function? You need to determine the most efficient path for securing sales.

At USI we recognized the importance of developing face-to-face customer relationships for real estate outsourcing services. Our direct sales force was one of the keys to our long-term success. Since the salesperson was the direct link to our target customer, USI invested in recruiting the best talent to build our sales team. We became a sales-driven company and built a sales platform responsible for all of the following activities:

- Developing and pursuing sales leads

- Separating qualified buyers from window shoppers

- Developing sales tools and tailored presentations

- Conducting sales meetings with target customers

- Generating pre-emptive proposals

- Responding to Requests for Proposals (RFPs)

- Finding solutions to complex customer problems

- Signing contracts and closing sales

- Continuously updating the Customer Relationship Management (CRM) system

- Building deep customer relationships

- Influencing new product development

- Developing exclusive multi-year contracts

Your product will not sell itself. Investing in a sales platform tailored to your product is vital to your success. The sales platform you select will be influenced by the complexity of the sale, the amount of product customization required, customer buying habits, and competitive sales methods.

Building an effective sales platform contoured to your business goals is expensive and time consuming, but critically important. There are no short-cuts. Since your sales platform is the face of your organization to your target customer, you need to get it right.

Step 16 | Resource Requirements: *What will it take to develop, produce, distribute, and sell your product?* Generate · a comprehensive list of all the resources needed to enable successful liftoff and ongoing operations. Quantify the cost of all the required resources including human, material, equipment, space, services, and capital needs. Having this information will help you figure out what it will cost to launch and operate your business.

For USI, I knew the business model, how to implement it, and how to sell it. But I needed people to help me execute the work and manage the business. I also needed office space, equipment, and trusted professionals to advise me. I could estimate these costs pretty easily.

When you boil it down, most businesses do three things: source, execute, and manage. Utilizing this three-step format will help you quantify your resource requirements:

Sourcing New Business:

- How many sales people do you need to develop new business?

- How much will it cost in travel, materials, salary, commissions, and overhead to develop new business?

Executing Orders:

- How many people do you need to produce your product or deliver your service? Will you hire direct staff or contract with an outsource provider?

- For a manufacturing business, how much will it cost to produce your product in terms of raw materials, equipment, storage, distribution, salary and overhead?

- For a service business, how much will it cost to deliver your service in terms of travel, materials, salary, and overheads?

- For a technology business, how much will it cost to deliver your service in terms of hardware, software, networks, salary, and overhead?

Managing the Business:

- How many people do you need to manage, plan, and direct the business? What will your management team cost in salary and overhead?

- How many people do you need to administer the business? What will your administrative resources cost in salary and overhead?

- How much infrastructure do you need? What will you spend on space, furniture, office equipment, communications, etc.?

- How much money will you need for professional services such as legal, accounting, insurance, banking, and consultants?

Although this methodology is not exhaustive, it does provide a simple framework to quantify resource requirements and costs for business liftoff and ongoing operations.

Step 17 | Profit Validation: *Can you forecast a profit?* Simple "back of the envelope" calculations will demonstrate if your business model can generate a profit. The basics of making a profit come down to this simple formula: revenues - expenses = profit (or loss).

You can validate annual profit or loss by completing the following calculation:

- Projected revenues (average sale x projected number of annual sales) *minus*

- Projected cost of revenue (average cost of sale x projected number of annual sales) *minus*

- Overhead expenses *equals*

- Operating profit (or loss).

Since the primary revenue generator for USI was based on transaction fees, all I needed to do was project the number of real estate transactions that I could complete in my first year multiplied by an average transaction fee (20 transactions x $12,000 fee = $240,000 projected revenue).

For expenses, I estimated an average delivery cost for each transaction ($5,000 average delivery cost x 20 transactions = $100,000 projected expenses).

As a result, I calculated $240,000 revenue - $100,000 expenses would equal a gross profit of $140,000 in our first year.

I planned to control my overhead costs by eliminating my first year's salary, paying my partners with a combination of equity and a minimal salary, pre-paying a low-cost sublease that included furniture and equipment, and putting a cap on travel expenses. Taken together, I estimated that we would run up $80,000 in overhead expenses in our first year. By subtracting our overhead expenses from our gross profit, we were able to project an operating profit of $60,000. In actuality, we generated an operating profit of almost $200,000 in our first year.

Validating your profit potential is a quick test of business viability. It can also help you identify and resolve problems or motivate startup actions. Here is how our simple projections looked:

United Systems Integrators Corporation (USI)

Financial Projections (3 Years)

	Year 1	Year 2	Year 3
Revenues	$ 240,000	$ 960,000	$1,920,000
Cost of Revenues	100,000	400,000	800,000
Gross Profit	140,000	560,000	1,120,000
Overhead Expenses			
Salaries and Benefits	60,000	240,000	480,000
Sales and Marketing	10,000	40,000	80,000
General and Administrative	10,000	40,000	80,000
Research and Development	–	–	–
Total Overhead Expenses	80,000	320,000	640,000
Depreciation & Amortization	–	–	–
Total Expenses	80,000	320,000	640,000
Operating Profit	$ 60,000	$ 240,000	$ 480,000
Interest & Taxes	6,000	48,000	120,000
Net Profit (Loss)	$ 54,000	$ 192,000	$ 360,000

Section Three: Potential

Step 18 | **Financial Projections:** *How will you know when you will make a profit?* This is the point when you need to calculate more detailed, month-by-month estimates of how much you can sell, when you will sell it, and what you will charge. You also need to figure out the direct cost of generating your sales, and your total overhead expenses on a more granular basis for at least the first year of operations, or until you reach breakeven. These projections will show you when you will generate a profit.

Rather than USI's service-based model, let's take a look at a product-based model to broaden the variables that impact financial projections.

Methodology for Estimating Profit

Let's talk about costs first. The terms "expenses" and "costs" can be used interchangeably, and there are two types: direct and indirect. Try not to get hung up on details that can be addressed later. You will miss the mark if you over-invest your time in this exercise. Let me give you an example of how simple your calculations can be.

First, you should figure out your direct costs or cost of revenues (also known as cost of goods sold): What will your product cost to produce and distribute?

Second, you should figure out your indirect costs or overhead expenses: What are your management and sales costs (refer to Step #16: Resource Requirements for greater detail)?

Remember, at this stage all you need are rough estimates that you can put into a spreadsheet.

ESTIMATE UNIT COSTS

After some quick research you determine that the product will cost $70 per unit to produce and $30 per unit to distribute, or $100 total direct cost per unit ("cpu").

ESTIMATE PRODUCT SALES

Now that you've estimated your direct unit costs, it's time to tackle how many units you believe you will sell. These estimates affect both your direct costs and your revenues. You can think in terms of the number of units, but you also need to specify a time period. How many units can you sell daily, weekly, monthly, or annually? For example, I believe that I can sell 50 units per week or 200 units per month or 2,400 units per year in my first year of operation.

Then, let's calculate the total direct costs: $100 direct cost per unit x 2,400 units per year = $240,000 annual direct costs.

PRICE YOUR PRODUCT AND ESTIMATE REVENUES

Since units sold x price = revenues, you will need to determine the price you will charge for your product. For now, just look at two options: cost-plus or market price. Both of these options can be influenced by your product's value to the customer and what customers pay for similar products from competitors.

To calculate cost-plus pricing, figure that a typical markup for a high-value product can range from 50% to 100% (or substantially more for premium products). For this example, let's use assume a 60% markup to determine the price under a cost-plus model: $100 total cpu + 60% markup = $160 price per unit.

ESTIMATE YOUR OVERHEAD

Using your resource requirements estimate, you need to add up all your ongoing overhead costs including: salaries & benefits, sales & marketing expenses, general & administrative expenses, and research & development. In our example, overhead expenses total $160,000 in the first year.

SIMPLE CALCULATIONS

Now, you can figure out the total annual operating profit. Start by estimating revenues:

Price per unit x units sold per year = estimated revenues.

In our example, $160 price per unit x 2,400 units per year = $384,000 in total estimated revenues. Next, we should calculate total direct costs:

Cost per unit (production + distribution costs) x units per year = total direct costs

In our example, we have $100 cost per unit x 2,400 units per year = $240,000 total direct costs. The difference between the revenues and direct costs (or cost of revenues) is your gross profit:

Revenue – direct cost = gross profit

In our example, $384,000 in annual revenues - $240,000 in annual costs = $144,000 in annual gross profit. From there, you can determine if your gross profit covers your indirect (or overhead) costs:

Gross profit – indirect costs = operating profit (loss)

In our example, $144,000 is gross profit minus $168,000 in total expenses = ($24,000) operating loss. Unlike a service business with minimal direct costs, a product business has substantial direct costs. However, once the revenue engine ramps up and overhead stabilizes, a manufacturing business can generate substantial profits.

Here is how the three-year projections for the manufacturing business in our example look:

Manufacturing Startup

Financial Projections (3 Years)

	Year 1	Year 2	Year 3
Revenues	$ 384,000	$ 1,152,000	$ 3,456,000
Cost of Revenues	240,000	720,000	2,160,000
Gross Profit	**144,000**	**432,000**	**1,296,000**
Overhead Expenses			
Salaries and Benefits	100,000	200,000	600,000
Sales and Marketing	20,000	40,000	120,000
General and Administrative	30,000	60,000	180,000
Research and Development	10,000	20,000	60,000
Total Overhead Expenses	**160,000**	**320,000**	**960,000**
Depreciation & Amortization	8,000	12,000	16,000
Total Expenses	**168,000**	**332,000**	**976,000**
Operating Profit	**$ (24,000)**	**$ 100,000**	**$ 320,000**
Interest & Taxes	–	9,600	100,800
Net Profit (Loss)	**$ (24,000)**	**$ 90,400**	**$ 219,200**

You will need to generate projections to make sure you can achieve your minimum profit objectives and to secure funding. To determine how your financial outlook will improve during your first year, fill out a spreadsheet on a month-by-month basis, using reasonable estimates for sales growth with proportional costs to support the growth.

Asking yourself if you can make a profit within your first 18 months of operation is a vital gut-check to make a decision whether or not to move forward. Exceptions include technology and biotech startups because of the amount of capital and extended timeframes needed to reach profitability.

Step 19 | **Cash Flow: *Will you have enough cash?*** Using your projections and estimates of your resource requirements, you can forecast how much cash you will spend monthly, commonly referred to as your monthly burn rate. Using best, likely, and worst-case scenarios, figure out the point at which the business will generate more cash than it burns. Use the results to understand how much cash to set aside to cover your expenses until you generate positive cash flow.

Even though I knew that any contracts USI would bring in could have a big payoff, I couldn't count on generating enough recurring revenue to cover all my operating costs upfront. Because I was planning to bootstrap the business, I wanted to be very conservative so I would not worry about running out of cash while we ramped up. This forced me to figure out a worse-case scenario and set aside $100,000 of my own money to fund startup costs and any contingencies.

To get a handle on your cash needs, some of the questions to consider include:

- What will you spend before starting operations?
- What will it cost to launch?
- How much will you spend on creating a prototype or samples to generate pre-sales?
- If you have to produce and store inventory before customers pay for it, how much will that cost?

- If you have to make a capital expenditure to purchase a plant or equipment, how much will it be?

- How fast will you burn through your cash?

- When will operating profits contribute to your bank account?

Having the answers to these questions before you launch will enable a successful liftoff. It doesn't matter if you're going to seek outside investors or if you are investing in yourself by bootstrapping; it's essential to have a handle on what it will take – and how long it will take – to turn the corner to profitability and achieve positive cash flow.

Keep in mind, operating cash flow is the key metric investors analyze to make funding decisions. Operating cash flow is also known as Earnings Before Interest, Taxes, Depreciation and Amortization, or EBITDA.

Step 20 | Management Team: *How will you manage your business?* Your startup will have lots of moving parts, requiring people with differing expertise to fulfill your vision. Think through what you can do yourself, and then bring in a team with complementary skills to get the job done.

I knew I needed a team to help me launch and grow USI. I had learned over the years that teams tend to create more value than individuals. If you are intent on creating a scalable business, you'll quickly realize that you cannot do it by yourself. You will need to recruit and hire people whom you can trust, the kind of people who can help you strategize, innovate, execute, and – when things look their darkest – commiserate and overcome challenges together.

To decide who will be on your team, you should ask yourself these questions:

■ Who will lead? Who will sell? Who will execute?

■ What value or competence do you bring to the business?

■ What will be your role and responsibility?

■ What additional value or competence is needed?

■ What roles and responsibilities need to be filled?

■ Who will complement your operating style?

■ Who will work with you 24/7 to fulfill the vision?

Then, ask yourself if you know people you can trust to fill the roles. If you cannot identify trusted partners, you will need to develop a personalized recruitment plan utilizing your network of trusted friends and associates.

Step 21 ┃ **Future Growth:** *How will you expand the business and your bottom line?* Do you have a strategic vision for growth? Do you have a plan to scale the business? To realize the full potential of your business, you need to develop a viable expansion plan to increase revenues and profits.

USI provided a family of integrated real estate, management, and information services in response to evolving customer outsourcing needs. Our growth strategy included customer relationship expansion, new service lines, new markets including global expansion, formation of specialized partnerships, and limited strategic acquisitions. All of the following strategies can contribute to your growth:

Customer Growth:

■ Expand existing customer accounts

■ Establish account profit centers to drive growth

- Develop new customer accounts
- Provide credit to finance customer purchases

Product Growth:

- Expand existing product lines
- Create new products and services
- Develop product bundles
- Establish product line profit centers

Geographic Growth:

- Expand geographically to open new markets
- Establish geographic profit centers
- Develop global expansion plans

Corporate Growth:

- Recruit and hire specialized leadership talent
- Create innovation centers
- Consider strategic partnerships
- Assess mergers and acquisitions

Your startup should be focused on survival, profitability, and cash flow. Once your business has been established, you can start to develop a strategic growth plan.

THE PURPOSE IS PROFIT

THE TRUTH ABOUT STARTING AND BUILDING YOUR OWN BUSINESS

By Ed McLaughlin

Wyn Lydecker
and Paul McLaughlin

BLUE
SUNSETS
BOOKS

ABOUT THE PURPOSE IS PROFIT

Unlike visionary "change the world" books, *The Purpose Is Profit* is for every one of you with the desire to start your own business – no matter the size, type, or scope. *The Purpose Is Profit* uses a personal story to describe the mental struggle to start up, the funding challenge, lessons learned from good and bad decisions, the scaling process to Inc. 500, and the sale to a Fortune 100 company. It is a realistic exposé of what worked and what didn't. *The Startup Roadmap: 21 Steps to Profitability* is also included in the full release of the book.

The following preview discusses An Entrepreneur's Motivation. It puts you in the shoes of an entrepreneur preparing to take the risk to start up and then provides chapter previews outlining the journey from startup to exit.

We hope you will read it and let us know what you think. You can email us at: ed@thepurposeisprofit.com to share your feedback and comments.

The Purpose Is Profit is scheduled for distribution in January 2016.

AN ENTREPRENEUR'S MOTIVATION

INTRODUCTION

People told me I was crazy. "You are going to fail!"

I can't blame my colleagues for saying that. I was setting out to start not one, but two, real-estate-related businesses in the midst of the major 1991 commercial real estate slump, brought on by the sweeping failures of savings and loans across the country. But I just had to do it. My heart told me the restrictions of a large corporation posed greater risk to my well-being than the uncertainty of starting my own venture. As it turned out, one of my businesses did fail. But the other one took off, generating a profit in its fourth month. My partners and I never looked back.

My purpose in writing this book is to eliminate the mystery of becoming an entrepreneur by sharing my experience and the principles I've learned from both failure and success. You, too, can conquer the fears holding you captive, preventing you from starting your own business. I hope my story will motivate those of you who are asking, "Should I look for a job or create my own job? Should I stay in the confines of my corporate position, or should I start a business of my own? Do I have what it takes to blast through the obstacles and risk it all?"

I was on the fast track, working for some of America's best managed corporations, including IBM, Hewlett-Packard, and Trammell Crow Company. Still, something was missing. I was selling their products and services, when I really wanted to create and sell my own. I was hungry for independent success and control. I yearned to hold out my ideas for the world to validate. I know these sentiments are not unique.

I resolved not to go to my grave without first starting my own business. But I had questions. What type of business would it be? What would be my product? How would I make money? Who would be my customer? I thought up different business models and new ideas every week for years. But when was it going to happen? I finally documented my commitment to start my own business by writing out a promise to myself, signing it in front of a witness, and carrying it in my wallet for years. I knew if I wrote down my desire as a covenant, I would make it happen.

Even while rising through the ranks of some of the nation's most respected corporations, I was growing tired of being told what to do, when to do it, and how to do it – especially when I knew there was a better way. Conforming to individual decisions driven by politics and having others decide where I fit in the pay-grade hierarchy was not my idea of the best way to make a living. Would my life just go on and on, tied to an income stream driven by the motivations of others? No. I wanted to take control of the mission for my life.

This book is all about that alternative path. If you do not like the choice of working for BigCo, then start NewCo. You will set the pace, the tone, and the direction. You will make the decisions, and you will be responsible for the outcomes. Yes, there is the risk of failure – but that is precisely why I have written this book. If you can understand the levers and gears within the startup machine, you can dramatically increase your probability of success.

Rather than a textbook approach, I want to share my startup experience by telling you the story of my journey, enumerating the principles of success and the hard lessons learned along the way.

I bootstrapped two companies at the same time: one startup was a passion project filled with promise that ended in commercial failure. The other startup not only thrived, it became an Inc. 500 Company and went on to be sold to a Fortune 100 Company. I want you to learn from both of these stories.

The essential difference between the two businesses was my distinctive competence. Distinctive competence is an exceptional skill or talent, specialized knowledge, and a record of achievement you've acquired through your unique experience. Having distinctive competence is Lesson #1: A venture filled with passion is not enough; you will substantially increase your probability of startup success if you build a business that leverages your distinctive competence.

■　■　■　■

Let me set the stage for my liftoff as an entrepreneur. It was 1990. I was 36 years old, married with two young children and working for Trammell Crow Company, the largest U.S. real estate developer. Trammell Crow paid me a good salary, but the industry was in turmoil. The traditional real estate development side of TCC was struggling for survival, and heads were starting to roll. On the other hand, our new service side was making money. Since the development side controlled the service side, there was tremendous political and performance pressure within TCC. This created trust issues around career, compensation, and control. My solution to this problem was always the same: out-perform my goals.

By the summer of 1990, I became the top producer for our business unit by landing what was lauded as the "mother lode" within the commercial real estate industry. It was the first comprehensive outsourcing contract for all corporate real estate service lines for a Fortune 100 company called Baxter International.

Even though it was a time to celebrate the Baxter victory, economic and internal political pressures were bearing down. TCC wanted to change my compensation package. Under duress, I agreed to accept a cut in compensation, with the understanding that I would be promoted to partner. My boss toasted my promotion with Champagne at the holiday party in December – but the other shoe was about to drop.

Fast-forward three months to one fateful Saturday morning in March of 1991. I had been out of town all week, so I went into the office that weekend to clean up some paperwork. When I walked into the copy room, a spreadsheet sat on top of the copying machine. Unintended for my eyes, it outlined three go-forward scenarios for our business unit: two of the three scenarios had me cut from staff.

That defining moment in the copy room pushed me with two hands to take the leap to start my own business.

Chapter 1

THE PULL AND THE PUSH

People normally say, "Push and pull," but every entrepreneur I've known has first faced the pull, and then the push.

The pull is the overwhelming desire to realize your own business vision. It is a mindset, a fire burning within you, and a relentless force like gravity. It is the knowledge deep within your soul that you will never be satisfied, and life will never feel complete, unless you start your own business.

The push is the crystallizing moment when your need to start your business becomes greater than the fear of venturing out on your own. It is the realization that you cannot work another day for someone else. Often, the push comes from an outside force that can literally shove you into becoming an entrepreneur.

For me, the final push was a long time coming.

I first felt the pull of entrepreneurship in 1976, the summer our nation celebrated its Bicentennial. I was a teenage lifeguard on the Jersey Shore. My days consisted of long spells sitting in the lifeguard chair watching people diving through the surf, playing on the sand, or swimming beyond the breakers.

While the public's safety was my main concern, sometimes to keep my mind active I thought up new business ideas.

Scientists had just begun to issue research reports warning too much sun exposure caused aging, wrinkles, and skin cancer. Repeated deep sunburns were particularly dangerous. With zinc-oxide streaked across my nose, I listened to these reports, and it hit me: Why not market a product to protect the skin from the sun's damaging rays? "Sunguard. From the People Who Know the Sun!"

Ed and Don lifeguarding on the Jersey Shore

My friend and fellow guard, Don Froude, and I got together every day after our shift and worked on the idea. When I told my father, he thought our concept was so good that he sent us to see his lawyer to get advice on how to proceed. My father made it clear that we had to pay the legal fees ourselves.

That was okay with me. It felt great to be taken seriously. I couldn't believe that we were meeting with a bona fide attorney. The lawyer set us up with a patent attorney who gave us an education about producing a skin lotion.

"You know, any time you develop a product that is going to go on your skin, you need to deal with the FDA. You need to test it to make sure it's safe. And you'll need to patent your formulation," the attorney said.

But somehow, we were not dismayed or overwhelmed. Don and I spent hours coming up with advertising ideas and even looking for a chemist until we headed off to college at summer's end. Although we never did start the business, our investment in Sunguard was time and money well spent. It educated us and lit the entrepreneurial fire, which was now burning within me, exerting its inexorable pull toward a goal of starting my own business.

The Pull Continues

My college years at Holy Cross in Worcester, Massachusetts, reinforced the lessons of ethics and integrity my family had taught me. The breadth of a liberal arts education, combined with a sense of accountability and debate, challenged me to consider the ramifications of my decisions. While Holy Cross lacked a professional business program, it provided a framework for sound judgment and sensitivity to the needs of others that has stayed with me.

Without a business education, I tried to figure out how to launch my career. Every adult I asked, including some professors, advised me to get my MBA or go to work for a top corporation with a formal training program to learn about business.

I didn't waste any time. Even before graduation, I had lined up a job with IBM. In the late 1970s, IBM had the best training program of any company in the country. I was certain that IBM would provide me with the experience and knowledge I needed.

Two years at IBM not only taught me how to sell, but also about life in a huge corporation. Looking back, I now appreciate how fortunate I was to be introduced to the "IBM Way." I learned how to develop a comprehensive value proposition and how to sell it to customers. In fact, IBM's sales techniques, discussed in detail in Chapter 9, still serve me today.

But I also learned that I was not going to be happy in an environment that controlled almost everything about my life: how to dress, how your pay grade affects your status, which country club to join. I decided to leave for another technology firm, Hewlett Packard (HP), because they had a more entrepreneurial reputation. HP, after all, had famously started in a Silicon Valley garage. And although the pull had a hold of me, I still felt the need to learn more about the world of business before starting my own venture.

The HP sales operation that hired me was located just outside Dallas, Texas, in a warehouse-like building, sitting out on the plains. HP was run by engineers more concerned about investing in new product innovation than spending money on a fancy office environment.

HP's business culture particularly appealed to me because it gave people enough rope to be innovative in their jobs. "Just don't hang yourself," my manager warned. Here was an environment where I could fit in and flourish.

My personal life also improved. Before long, I met and married Barbara Boyd. Barbara had recently graduated from Baylor Dental School in Dallas and started her own dental practice. Sure enough, she was living my dream, running her own business. Every night we discussed her business challenges and growth opportunities. Attracting new patients was the lifeblood of a new dental practice. We spent hours talking about marketing programs that would rapidly build a clientele.

Finally, the idea struck: "Gentle Dentistry" would become the theme for her marketing program (although this mantra is more common today, it was a breakthrough concept in the early 1980s). Barbara created a successful "Gentle Dentistry" direct-mail marketing campaign. Soon her practice was booming – until she received a cease-and-desist letter from the state dental board. You see, they didn't like the implication that Barbara's dentistry was gentle, while other dentists were painful. Oh well, at least Barbara got the benefit of the Gentle Dentistry campaign while it lasted.

Although Barbara was open to my ideas and inputs, she started to realize that I was trying to relieve my new business frustrations through her dental practice. Everything came to a head on our monthly drive to Arkansas to visit her folks. Can you imagine getting an earful of business development strategy for seven straight hours while trapped in a car? As soon as we left Dallas, I'd start in on all the ways she could improve her business, from back-office management to marketing to bringing in more patients.

Finally, on one of those long drives, Barbara turned to me and said, "You know, Ed, you really ought to start your own business." With a bit of sarcasm, she added, "You can take all that energy you have and put it into something of your own."

She was right. Instead of having the guts to start my own business, I was acting the part of an entrepreneur vicariously through her business. I'd wake up in the middle of the night thinking about how much I wanted to run my own show, to make my own decisions, and to live or die by them. I spent hours tossing around new business ideas – so much so that I became frustrated, anxious, and impatient. I was passionate about starting something, and Barbara was giving me the first of several small pushes. Yet, I still lacked the confidence, the competence, and the big idea I knew were crucial for launching a successful business.

The Promise

Then one day when I was feeling particularly frustrated about my career, I had lunch with a trusted friend and respected advisor. Her name was Annette Field. Our conversation turned to my job and the plans I had for my future. Over the years, I had consulted with Annette on everything from my personal goals to purchasing my engagement ring.

She looked me straight in the eye. "Are you happy, Ed?" Annette asked. "Where do you want to go with your career? What are you doing about it?'

When I laid out my desire to start my own business, Annette told me that one of her sons, who was my age, had left a big accounting firm to start his own practice. "He is very successful and truly happy – far happier than he ever was working for someone else."

The discussion hit a nerve. When we got back to her office, I asked Annette for a piece of paper, took out a pen, and wrote down a promise to myself that I would start a business within the next five years. Then I signed it and asked Annette to add her signature as my witness.

Once I had that paper in my wallet, I was finally able to sleep at night.

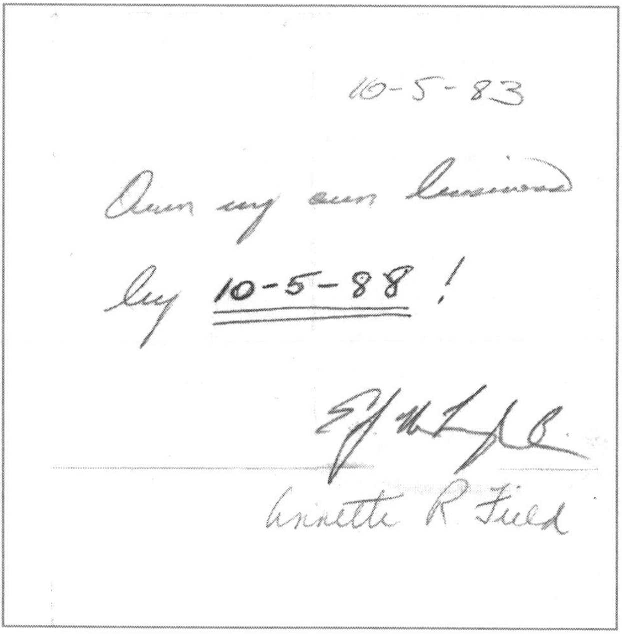

10-5-83

[handwritten text]

10-5-88 !

[handwritten signature]

Annette R. Field

The Promise

If you're feeling the pull toward the entrepreneurial life, sit down and craft a covenant. Document your goal to start up a business, and sign it in front of a trusted friend. It can make all the difference. Although I did not formally launch my business until 1991, documenting my startup commitment resolved my internal conflict and memorialized my plans for startup.

My promise was in my pocket when I went into work at HP one Saturday. Coming out of the Texas heat, I entered our air-conditioned building and walked into our cavernous sales arena. As I looked across the sea of empty desks, a senior HP sales executive and mentor spotted me and came over.

"Ed, if you're going to work this hard," he said, "then you should be working for your own account. You'll only realize the real benefit of all your efforts that way."

I distinctly remember my response, "I'm dying to start my own business. I just don't know what kind of business it should be."

"You can make so much more money, have so much more control, and have so much more freedom in the long run," my mentor said.

Here, a man I respected had just validated my burning desire and given me yet another push. What was holding me back?

The Pull Leads to a New Direction

As I wondered what sort of business I should start, I saw people in Texas reshaping the suburban landscape. Many of them were my peers. Previously, most large office buildings had been in central business districts, with the majority in downtowns. Now office space was sprouting up all over, even in rural areas. I realized that I wanted to be part of this growing industry – commercial real estate.

An old friend, former HP colleague, and recent Harvard Business School graduate, Henry Johnson, had just joined Trammell Crow Company, the nation's largest commercial real estate developer. TCC had hired Henry in their Dallas headquarters to help start a new division called Trammell Crow National Marketing (TCNM). The division would sell and lease TCC's real estate directly to 30 designated accounts within the Fortune 500.

Traditionally, real estate firms were organized in local markets, waiting for corporations to come to them when they had a real estate need. Transactions happened only at the local level. But this new division would go out and ask for the order from the source at national headquarters.

Henry called me up and said, "You need to be part of this." He told me I could be a significant contributor in this new startup group.

The offer was irresistible. I said to myself, I'm going for it!

Now, I would be part of something small, new, and growing, partly satisfying the entrepreneurial pull. As a sales executive with TCNM, I traveled to my assigned accounts in the Midwest to cultivate relationships with their corporate real estate departments. We set out to become the corporation's single point of contact for commercial real estate.

Trammell Crow National Marketing was highly competitive and focused on results. Their aggressive reward system fed these goals.

This entrepreneurial environment within a larger enterprise began to satisfy my hunger to create genuine value. Our small real estate services division started to add meaningful revenue and profit to Trammell Crow's bottom line. As we grew the business, we expanded into the lucrative Northeast Corridor, crowded with the headquarters of the majority of the Fortune 100 Companies.

I relocated from Dallas to Stamford, Connecticut, and worked my way up and became the top rainmaker. After two years of dedicated work, I brought in the single largest real estate services deal ever completed. The contract comprised the complete and exclusive re-engineering of Baxter Healthcare's distribution centers. That experience was exhilarating and kept my entrepreneurial fires stoked.

I had worked hand-in-hand with my customer, Bill Agnello, who was Baxter's Vice President of Real Estate, to develop a system that could manage the consolidation of all Baxter's distribution centers after the firm had acquired American Hospital Supply. At that point, no other healthcare supply company had more distribution space. We had to find a way to eliminate redundancies while expanding Baxter's distribution network.

Bill and Ed

To accomplish these goals, we utilized Baxter's business framework, which they labeled "Value-Managed Relationships." This relationship structure connected Baxter and TCC around a common management system responsible for delivering hard savings, increased flexibility, consistent quality, and access to specialized resources with superior execution. Essentially, we reinvented the entire real estate delivery system for Baxter, which grew to include the comprehensive outsourcing of all real estate projects and personnel to Trammell Crow. As a result of the Baxter outsourcing contract, TCNM was rebranded Trammell Crow Corporate Services, and the division transitioned from a marketing arm to a full-fledged profit center.

The Baxter deal woke me up. It clearly showed me that I could create a new way of doing business and deliver genuine value to corporations by serving their real estate and facilities management needs. This new-found knowledge made me realize that I had a distinctive competence that I could bank on to start my own business. As you will read in Chapter 2, distinctive competence is a combination of unique skills, experience, and knowledge you have acquired over time.

This feeling of having a distinctive competence was exactly what I had been seeking. It made me realize that the pull of entrepreneurship was now a realistic dream.

The Push

As a result of what we had accomplished with Baxter, Trammell Crow Corporate Services was no longer something small and entrepreneurial. Our division was delivering significant profits to the company's bottom line. As a result, the political pressure around compensation and control became a big issue and began to wear on me.

Concurrent with the explosive growth in corporate services, the real estate development business was in free fall. The incredible expansion in development that had initially excited me was turning into a massive oversupply. The nation's economy – and commercial real estate in particular – was in a downward spiral. These factors made the environment at Trammell Crow turn darker.

At the office, I sensed the need to keep looking over my shoulder, watching what I said, and feeling as though I needed to kowtow to the people above me. My productivity suffered because I felt I could not trust the system, and my heart was not in my work.

In the midst of all this, it became clear that our division's success had become the envy of the faltering development side.

The services division had been subordinate to the larger, more profitable development business. Suddenly the roles were reversed. The service business was positioned to become the future of the company, which rankled the interests of some of the leadership. This shift in power created tremendous pressure within our group.

The tensions around compensation and control continued to mount. Even though Trammell Crow made me a partner, the promotion came at the cost of being forced to accept a reduction to my compensation. A few months later, when I found the spreadsheet in the copy room that showed scenarios cutting me from staff, it became clear that my efforts and approach were not valued by everyone in the hierarchy.

I was stunned. How could a newly minted partner, who had just landed the largest real estate outsourcing deal in history, be targeted for elimination? I felt blindsided and completely disillusioned. The whole incident stabbed at the heart of my loyalty. There was no turning back. This was the final big push.

My time had come. I was going to take control and start up. I was going to build a business where integrity, hard work, and creating value were rewarded more than playing politics. At the same time, I recognized my distinctive competence would enable me to be the architect of a new business model, figure out how all the pieces fit together, and create value for corporate clients. If the outsourcing value proposition had worked for Baxter, there was no reason that it would not work for many other corporations.

I began to plot my course to build a corporate real estate outsourcing business. At the same time, I conceived a second new business to address the over-supply of commercial real estate from the S&L crisis. It seemed every corporation and institution were flooded with surplus real estate. If I could help solve this vexing problem, I felt I could meet my customers' greatest need, build a defensible business, and generate substantial profits.

My plan was to develop and produce a publication that included a compendium of surplus real estate for corporations and institutions to create a global market for buyers and sellers. Even though I became enamored with the idea of the publication, I had to acknowledge my lack of experience and expertise in the field. Given the scale and scope of this publishing venture, and knowing that my distinctive competence lay in developing and selling outsourcing services, I decided to focus on the outsourcing business first. Once the services business was established, I would start the publication as a second step. The publication became my passion project, the subject of Chapter 8.

Acknowledge the Pull, and Accept the Push

Working for myself has been far more exciting and rewarding than anything else I have ever done. In the rest of this book, you'll see how I finally started my business and turned it into a multi-million dollar enterprise. It all started with that promise in my pocket: I will start my own business.

Acknowledging the pull is becoming aware of an unserved need or an existing imperfection, coupled with a burning desire to do something about it. Accepting the push is more difficult than acknowledging the pull. The push is the realization that no matter how hard you work, how much you produce, and how much value you create, you cannot change the hierarchy, the politics, and the motivations of those who control your fate.

The Pull

- Are you dying to take control of your own destiny?

- Do you have a great idea for how to fill a real need?

- Do you believe your idea could transform lives for the better or disrupt the way business is done?

- Do you have a special talent that friends tell you to use to start a business?

- Do you have a unique competence in an area that you can use to create a business?

- Do you want to disrupt the status quo with a new product or service?

- Do you want to leave your mark on the world?

- Are you on fire to start your own business?

The Push

- Are you tired of working for someone else, being told what to do, and precisely how to do it?

- Have you lost your trust in "the system"?

- Does Human Resources make you feel like a replaceable part?

- Have you been waiting in line, answering ads, attending interviews but never landing an actual job?

- Are you looking over your shoulder in fear at work?

- Have you had enough of playing the game by other people's rules?

- Are you dying to make your own rules and create your own business culture?

THE PURPOSE IS PROFIT CHAPTER PREVIEWS

Introduction

Section One: PRE-LAUNCH

Chapter 1: The Pull and the Push

The pull is the overwhelming desire to realize your own business vision, to be in charge of your own destiny. Whereas, the push is the crystallizing moment when your need to start your business becomes greater than the fear of venturing out on your own.

Chapter 2: Distinctive Competence

You will substantially increase your probability of startup success if you build a business in which you have distinctive competence. What special knowledge, exceptional talent, or unique skill can you bring to your business?

Chapter 3: Dynamic Planning

When starting a business you need to organize your thoughts, goals, strategies, and plans so that you can realize your business vision – all while dealing with the nonstop challenges of launching. I call this active process dynamic planning.

Section Two: LAUNCH AND EARLY STAGE

Chapter 4: Entrepreneurial Branding

The difference between traditional corporate branding and entrepreneurial branding is two-fold: first, the brand is a highly personal reflection of you and your vision, and second, you must take full responsibility for all facets of the branding process.

Chapter 5: Startup Funding

Every business needs capital to start, operate, and grow. You need to decide if you will use other people's money or your own money. I believe bootstrapping is best.

Chapter 6: Capital, Cost and Control

How much capital do you really need? What is the true cost of the capital you are seeking? How can you minimize your risk while maximizing control?

Chapter 7: Do It! Do It! Do It!

It is time to put your plans into action. "Do It! Do It! Do It! You can build more wealth and have more fun than a lifetime spent in the corporate world."

Chapter 8: The Passion Project

Blinded by passion and without a shred of proven competence, I launched a national magazine within 12 months of my first startup. The publication bled red ink for more than three years before shutting down. This venture demonstrates that passion is not enough; you really need distinctive competence to create a successful business.

Section Three: GROWTH STAGE

Chapter 9: Sales Is a Contact Sport
Like high-performance athletes, we developed a mindset that we deserved to win every contest. We described our competitive drive by coining the phrase: Sales is a Contact Sport. You can start a business, produce a great product, and offer a superior value proposition, but you need to invest in a professional sales force to ensure your success.

Chapter 10: The Ten Commandments of Startup Profit
From the beginning, we were organized around 10 core profit principles. We factored profit into every business decision that we made. These 10 profit principles get at the nub of how USI made consistent profits and how they can help you produce sustainable profits as well.

Section Four: EXIT

Chapter 11: Realizing Value
With market pressure looming on the horizon, we decided it was time to sell the company. As we reviewed the proposals, I began to realize that my small startup had grown into a valuable company. We could monetize our equity at peak value, and the entire firm could be vaulted into a new, more powerful position. You can take a seat at the negotiating table with a Fortune 100 company and gain the insider's perspective on how we maximized our valuation.

Chapter 12: Preserving the Secret Sauce
Even though the company that bought us wanted to preserve the secret sauce, I soon realized it was on their

terms and under their direction. Selling your business can create a substantial windfall, but it will come at the price of control. You need to think beyond the obvious strategic benefits and visualize the operating realities of your life after the sale.

Epilogue: To Thine Own Self Be True

As I approached the end of my stay-back period, I realized that my first love was entrepreneurship. I just had to step away from the big corporate life and return to my entrepreneurial roots. So I started a new business and continue to use the profit principles in this book as an entrepreneur and angel investor today.

About the Authors

Ed McLaughlin | Ed is the founder of four businesses. Ed bootstrapped USI Companies and grew it into an Inc. 500 company and was honored as Entrepreneur of the Year by Ernst and Young. In 2005, he sold USI to Johnson Controls, a Fortune 100 Company. Ed then became CEO of JCI's Global Workplace Business for the Americas. Ed is currently running his fourth company, Blue Sunsets LLC, investing in startups and real estate. He has a BA from the College of the Holy Cross. Active in philanthropy, Ed lives with his wife in Connecticut and has three adult children.
EMAIL: ed@thepurposeisprofit.com
LINKEDIN: www.linkedin.com/in/edskipmclaughlin
WEBSITE/BLOG: www.thepurposeisprofit.com

Wyn Lydecker | Wyn is the founder of Upstart Business Planning. She works with entrepreneurs to develop plans that answer the questions investors ask most often. She has an MBA in Finance and Marketing from the Wharton School of the University of Pennsylvania and a BA in Economics from the University of California at Santa Barbara. She lives in Connecticut with her husband and has two adult children.
EMAIL: wyn@thepurposeisprofit.com
LINKEDIN: www.linkedin.com/in/wynlydecker

Paul McLaughlin | Paul is pursuing his MBA at Georgetown's McDonough School of Business. Paul served as Vice President of Blue Sunsets LLC, where he was responsible for real estate development and specific angel investments. He has a BA in Mathematics from the College of the Holy Cross.

EMAIL: paul@thepurposeisprofit.com
LINKEDIN: www.linkedin.com/in/paulpmclaughlin

The Purpose Is Profit is Scheduled
for Release in January 2016.

***The Purpose Is Profit* will:**

- Eliminate the mystery of becoming an entrepreneur
- Explain how to fund and grow your startup
- Focus you on generating profit from the get-go
- Enable you to build a business based on trust and integrity
- Give you a seat at the negotiating table with a Fortune 100 company

***The Purpose Is Profit* is designed to:**

- Empower frustrated corporate professionals to start up
- Excite enterprising students to become entrepreneurs
- Motivate millennials to become business builders
- Compel hungry empty-nesters to launch a business
- Inspire retired professionals to create a new venture

***The Purpose Is Profit* because:**

- Profit allows you to pay your bills and save
- Profit underwrites sustainable job creation
- Profit funds your growth and expansion
- Profit enables social responsibility and giving back
- Profit fuels the fulfillment of your business vision

Please email us at: ed@thepurposeisprofit.com to share your feedback and comments.

37520700R00049

Made in the USA
San Bernardino, CA
21 August 2016